MW00416201

Contents

~Dedicated to my amazing mum, who has given me the best guidance in life~

https://twitter.com/_worthyemily
https://verbalabusehelp.com/

I deserve to be loved

Introduction

I'm so glad you picked up this little book of self love. It is dedicated to all of us out there who need a boost and who would like to feel better about ourselves, our life, future and our relationships.

This book was created with care and thought to help build your self esteem and confidence during or after an emotional trauma or abusive relationship. It is designed to heal your heart and will put you in the right direction to help you feel better about yourself again. Don't forget what an amazing, unique and incredible person you are and that your life truly matters!

What are Positive Affirmations?

Affirmations are positive statements, words or phrases you tell yourself. They can help you build your self image, when you feel low or negative. You can give yourself encouragement and kind words to heal yourself and banish harmful thoughts from your mind, as soon as they appear. A meaningful change starts from inside your head and heart.

Repeat it, See it and be it!

Your subconscious stores emotions and information, which then reflects onto your self image and the way you feel about yourself. If you do not train your mind, it becomes what it is given from input you have heard throughout your life, from good teachers and encouraging friends. However, this can also mean that your mind retains criticism and unkind words from abusive and thoughtless people as well.

So how do you build up your image when you are feeling down? It is extremely valuable to counter disparaging thoughts with positive statements. You can use encouraging phrases to grow confidence and transform negative behaviour into positive ones. To sum it up, if you can repeat it and see it, then you can be it! Your imagination and visualisation can equal your reality.

Create your own Affirmations

You can either use the affirmations that I have created within my book, or make your own. If you want to make your own read the following!

Do you think more about pessimistic or encouraging thoughts? If your mind is constantly barraging you with negativity then that is a good place to start when thinking about constructive phrases to create for yourself.

Take a few minutes when you are on your own to think about that unfriendly, annoying chattering voice in your head that helps you keep that negative self image. What is it saying? This is what mine told me when I was in an abusive relationship and for years afterwards:-

"Emily, you need to make more of an effort! If you had worn a prettier dress, then he wouldn't have said you looked a mess."

"You won't achieve your goals, your partner said so. So why not give up? Just go watch some television instead!"

"Remember that mean comment last week? Perhaps they were right, you really are an idiot."

When you hear that voice, you can turn these negative thoughts into positive ones by spinning them on their head:-

"I make good choices and deserve respect"

"I have the power to achieve any goals that I set"

"I choose to ignore hurtful and unconstructive comments"

When writing your positive phrases, always keep to the following:-

- Present tense: Affirmations are always written as if they are happening right at this moment

- Personal achievement: Use phrases such as 'I am', 'I have', 'I accept', 'I am capable' and 'I deserve'. Eliminate words that are non-committal or downbeat, for example, 'might', 'want', 'should' or 'don't'.

- Positivity: Focus on what you are moving in the direction of, rather than what you want to leave behind.

- Predict your accomplishments: Include actions, such as 'quickly', 'effortlessly' and 'flourish'.

How to Use Your Affirmations

Write down your affirmations and put them in places where you will see them around the house or at work. Save the examples in my book as computer desktop backgrounds, flick through them on your digital reading app, take a copy of the book with you, or just simply write them on a post it note. I have a friend who has a chalkboard that she hangs in her kitchen and changes her affirmation according to her mood.

When you get up in the morning, say or read your chosen affirmations five times. Repeat this throughout the day, once again at lunchtime, in the evening and just before you go to sleep. Visualise and internalise your affirmations. Picture how you look as this confident, vibrant and productive person. Imagine you are feeling the emotions that you want to create for yourself!

You may find initially that your subconscious fights back and you have a battle going on in your head. That is normal, especially when you are on the receiving end of abuse. If you keep repeating your affirmations, the positive thoughts will win over the negative ones, I promise.

I hope you enjoy reading the following affirmations that I created. Feel free to use them in any way that you wish and share them with your friends!

Love and best wishes, Emily.

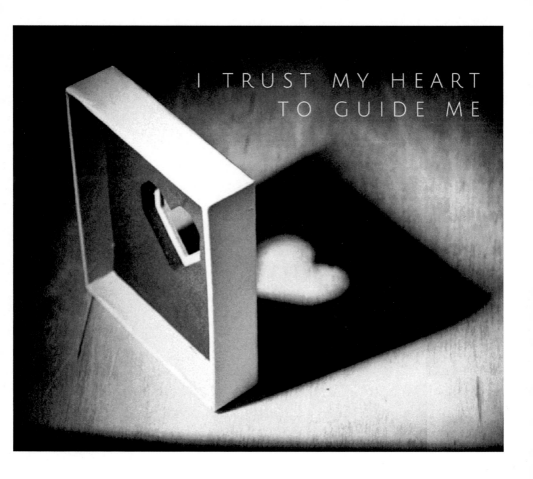

I TRUST MY HEART
TO GUIDE ME

66

I accept that I cannot change or control the people who hurt me

I let go
of any
patterns
that no longer
serve me

I surround
myself with
★ positive people ★
who appreciate
my light

I LOVE MYSELF UNCONDITIONALLY
JUST AS I AM.

I choose to respect and care for myself

I can say no to other people and still remain loved and cared for

I accept that I can only understand myself and my own behaviour

I

TRUST

MY

JUDGEMENT

COMPLETELY

I PICTURE MYSELF AS A STRONG AND
VIBRANT PERSON

I am beautiful inside and out

I AM WORTHY

I seek to live a nurturing and peaceful life

I give myself
permission to
take time out

I will create healthy boundaries for myself

I WILL NOT
SEEK OUT
RATIONAL
INTENTIONS
BEHIND
IRRATIONAL
WORDS

I am a valuable
and creative
person

I know that abuse is never my fault.

I deserve kindness and consideration at all times

I have the power
to change my life

I accept support
and understanding
from people who
care for me

I MAKE HEALTHY CHOICES FOR MY BODY AND MIND

I will thrive
without
negativity in my
life

my true self is emerging through my spiritual journey

I will guide myself
through darkness
by gaining
knowledge

Only I will define myself

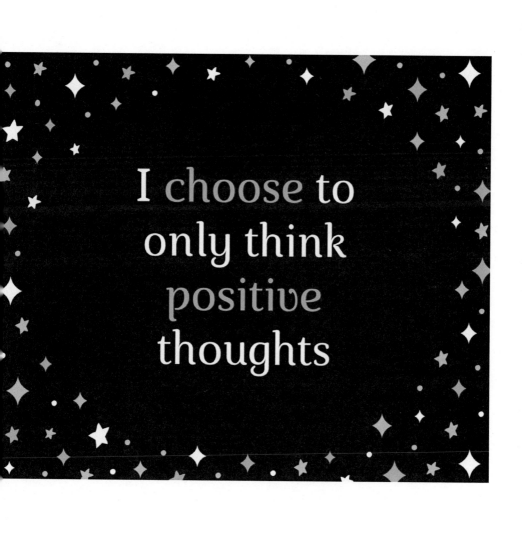

I am truly an amazing and unique person

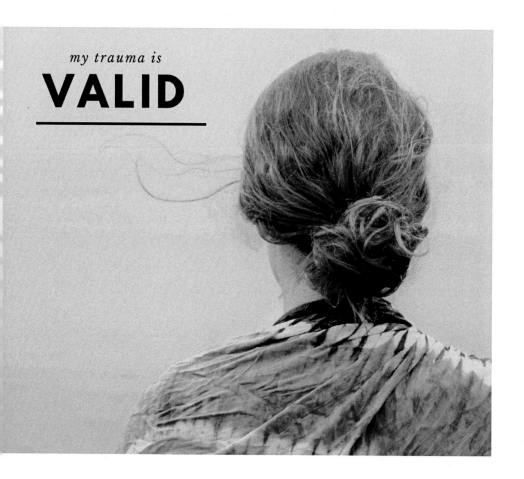

my trauma is
VALID

I deserve to be heard, understood, believed and supported

I'm taking small steps towards
a better life

I love and approve of myself.

My desire for love
and respect
is legitimate

The sounds of nature fill my heart, bringing me peace

I acknowledge my own self worth;
my confidence is soaring

I am always developing and growing

I will stop reliving
negative memories

I know that all types of abuse hurt equally

I deserve the best that life has to offer

I recognise
the great
qualities
that I have

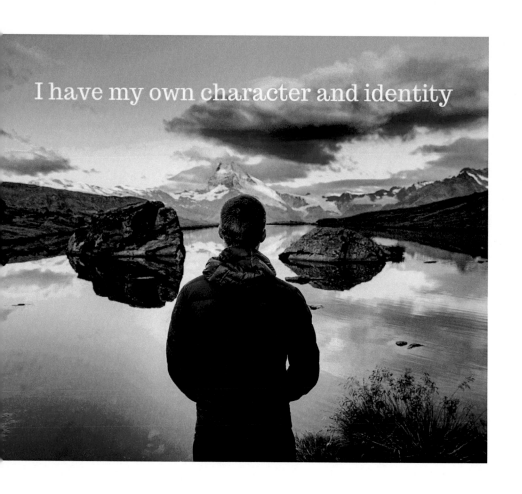

Nature is nurturing me, helping me flourish

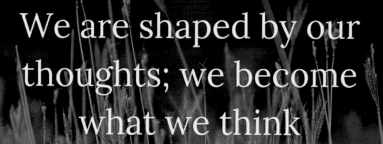

We are shaped by our thoughts; we become what we think

When the mind is pure, joy follows like a shadow that never leaves

BUDDHA

Before you go

Thank you so much for reading my book, I hope you have found my affirmations helpful. If you could take the time to write a review, I would be extremely grateful.

Other books in the my 'Little Book' series are:-

The Little Book of Sobriety - to help you if you want to recover from any addiction
https://goo.gl/VGjmYL

The Little Book of Successful Leadership: The Missing Piece of the Puzzle
https://goo.gl/blcVtK

Follow me on twitter:- https://twitter.com/_worthyemily

Alternatively, I would welcome any emails via emilyhayworth16@gmail.com.

Best wishes, Emily.

~with special thanks to Morris Coyle for his creative camera work and photography~

11309634R00035

Made in the USA
San Bernardino, CA
03 December 2018